Teaching Primary Math with Music

Grades K–3

Esther L. Mendlesohn

DALE SEYMOUR PUBLICATIONS

Dedicated to all the young children
who are just starting out on their
math adventures, with the hope
that happy beginnings will
lead to successful futures.

Cover design and illustrations: Rachel Gage

Order number DS01034
ISBN 0-86651-512-7

DALE
SEYMOUR
PUBLICATIONS
P.O. BOX 10888
PALO ALTO, CA 94303

2 3 4 5 6 7 8 9 10 11-MA-95 94 93 92

Contents

Introduction

To meet the demands of technology, the math curriculum has changed dramatically. In our schools we talk about calculators, computers, floppy disks, and software. Young students today need to be familiar with these high-tech tools. However, certain basic truths still apply. If we agree that children learn more readily when they're happy, then it's up to us as teachers to make a more pleasant, positive classroom atmosphere.

We know that one of the things most children love is music. What better classroom helper than a happy song that teaches, that brings into focus the very essence of a lesson and helps students remember what they've learned?

Teaching Primary Math with Music includes thirty enjoyable songs for use with the K–3 math curriculum. The choice is yours, depending upon your particular group's skill level and interest. You can use the songs to introduce or culminate a lesson, or both. They add interest to a lesson and always provide cheerful motivation to review and reinforce specific skills.

The songs in this book have been tested extensively in classrooms throughout the country and have been very effective in helping teach primary math. Classes have eagerly asked to sing "Five Steps to Problem Solving." Students have been seen on the playground jumping rope to some of these songs—and incidentally reinforcing their math lessons! One little girl from an inner-city school, instead of saying "hello," greeted me by singing, "When we subtract 'How many are left?' is the thing we want to know"—three years after she had learned the song! "I taught this song to my mother," she said proudly.

The songs in this book cover counting; addition; subtraction; early multiplication and division; telling time; money; beginning geometry; and measurement. Detailed "Notes to Teachers" accompany the songs. The book includes seven "Student Worksheet" blackline masters and eleven "Teacher Sheets," which contain lessons and blackline masters for other activities.

A cassette tape of the songs in this book is available. The tape can be a great help not only to teachers who don't play a musical instrument, but also to those who wish to point out examples or move around the room checking on students' work during a song.

Much incidental learning goes on in the classroom when we aren't actually teaching. You will enhance your use of any song by printing its lyrics on a large poster. This is especially valuable when teaching songs that include an algorithm, a series of steps for solving a problem. Students can read the words on the poster and also look for rhymes, or pick out action words (verbs) or names of things (nouns).

If, toward the end of the year, students have learned many of the songs, why not have a math assembly? Students can sing the songs as well as act them out for an unusual and successful program.

Many teachers have used these songs in their math lessons with great success and enjoyment, and you can, too. Here's to happy, successful teaching of primary math—with music! ♪

Teaching Primary Math with Music

We Use Numbers Every Day

Lively

We use num - bers e - very day, in our work and in our play.

1. What's the num - ber on your tel - e - phone? How much was that ice cream cone?
2. What's your fa - vorite chan - nel on T. V.? How ma - ny in your fam - i - ly?
3. When you write a let - ter, what's the zip? How ma - ny miles were on that trip?

Note to Teachers

This first song was written with the 1989 National Council of Teachers of Mathematics (NCTM) Curriculum Standards in mind, "to help children establish a link between their world and the world of numbers."

♪ Students can build language arts skills by making lists of other aspects of life that involve numbers.

♪ Students with advanced skills might make up new verses for the class to sing, or write stories featuring numbers.

♪ As a group or individually, younger students can dictate stories about numbers that the teacher can write down. Students can sign the stories and take them home.

♪ You might ask students to make four columns, with these headings: "How much?", "How many?", "How long?", and "How far?" Then have students come up with questions for each column that can be answered with a number, such as "(How much) does that book cost?" or "(How many) children are in the room?" Thinking about how often we ask questions like these will help reinforce the concept that "we use numbers every day."

At the ball game, what's the score? See all the price tags in the store!
What size sneak - ers do you wear? How ma - ny socks are in a pair? How
What's the time? and what's the date? Step on a scale and what's your weight?

much? How ma - ny? How long? How far? We use num - bers where - e - ver we are!

Up, Down, Left, and Right

To a march tempo

Up! Down! Left and right! Op-po-sites like day and night.
In and out we go. Op-po-sites like fast and slow.

Top, bot-tom, mid-dle, too. We know where they are. Do you?
O-ver and un-der, too. We know where they are. Do you?

Note to Teachers

The purpose of this song is to introduce opposite spatial relationships by having students experience them.

Sometimes younger students learn a concept when they feel it through body movement. By singing "up" while they reach their hands up, then singing "down" while putting their hands down, students can feel that "up" and "down" are opposites.

♪ The song's marching rhythm suggests a parade. After discussing the words and listening to the song, students can march to the song and act out the words.

♪ Introduce a language arts activity by asking students to suggest other opposites such as day and night, summer and winter, or black and white.

♪ Conduct a science activity in which students experience opposites such as hot and cold, wet and dry, rough and smooth, or bitter and sweet.

♪ In a related art activity, have students illustrate their experiences. They can create individual booklets to take home or combine for a class mural or bulletin board.

Counting to Ten

Note to Teachers

Kindergarten children are very proud of being able to count. "Counting to Ten" happily reinforces that skill through repetition.

♪ Students may sing the song as they march, stopping to emphasize the word *a-gain* before they continue. They may pause to sing about counting pennies and fingers, then continue marching to the counting part of the song.

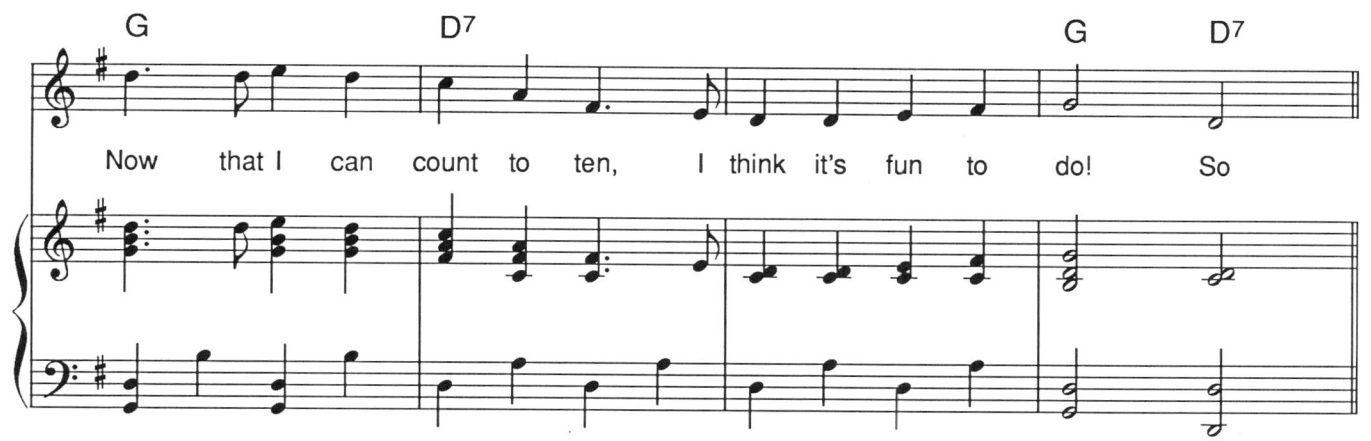

to the beginning

Now that I can count to ten, I think it's fun to do! So

And Then There Were Ten

Moderately

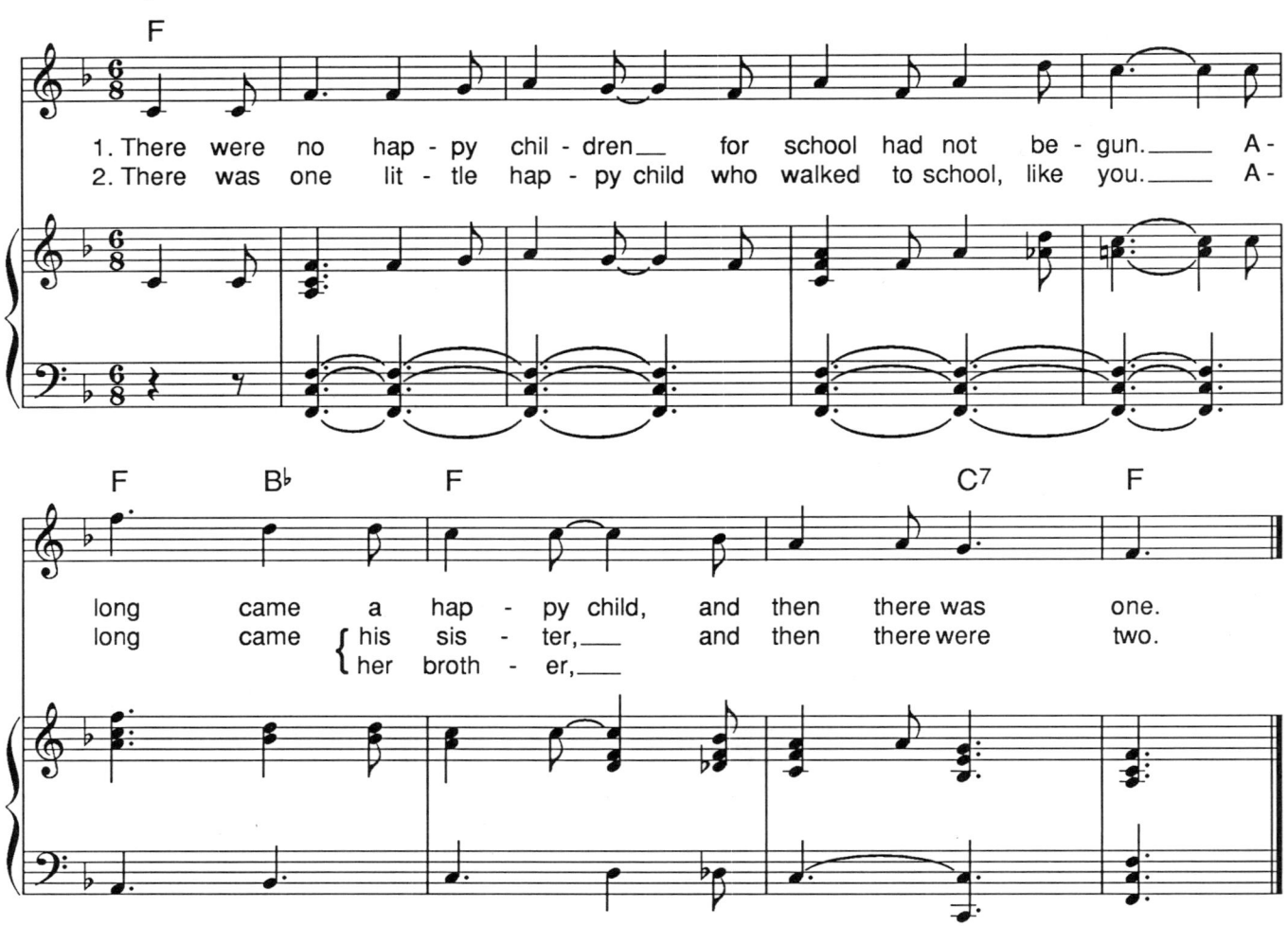

1. There were no hap - py chil - dren___ for school had not be - gun.___ A-			
2. There was one lit - tle hap - py child who walked to school, like you.___ A-			

long came a hap - py child, and then there was one.
long came { his sis - ter,___ and then there were two.
{ her broth - er,___

3.

There were two happy children
Who *hopped* around a tree.
Along came a friend of theirs
And then there were three.

4.

There were three happy children
Who *skipped* into a store.
Along came another friend,
And then there were four.

5.

There were four happy children
Who *ran* right past a hive!
Along came another friend
And then there were five.

6.

There were five happy children
Who *stooped* to pick up sticks.
Along came one more friend
And then there were six.

7.

There were six happy children
Who *jumped* way up toward heaven.
Along came another friend
And then there were seven.

8.

There were seven happy children
Now *hurry!* Don't be late!
Along came another friend
And then there were eight.

9.

There were eight happy children
Who *walked* to get in line.
Along came one more friend
And then there were nine.

10.

There were nine happy children
Who *heard* the bell, and then—
OUT came the teacher!
And then there were ten.

Note to Teachers

"And Then There Were Ten" develops the concepts of order and the number line and shows how they relate to each other. The number line is a graphic representation of order. By singing the story of children on their way to school along a number line, students can "feel" the concept of order developing.

♪ Have students follow along the number line on the *Order and the Number Line* Student Worksheet (page 10) while you play the song yourself or play the accompanying tape. You or an assistant can go about the room to watch each child's progress. Here is a sample of how this might be done:

Teacher: "We are going to follow some children on their way to school along a number line while we listen to a song about them."

(Start the song and stop it after "for school had not begun.")

"At the left end of the number line, marked A, put your finger on the zero. 'Zero' is the numeral we use when we want to show that there aren't any, and no children were on their way to school yet. Whenever you hear 'along came' in the song, move your finger to the next numeral."

(Play the song and stop after "and then there was one.")

"Did you move your finger to the numeral 1? If you haven't done so, do it now."

(Wait and check.)

"You should all be pointing to the numeral 1."

(Continue the song through the fifth verse and stop.)

"The next time you hear 'along came,' move your finger down to the beginning of the line marked B, to the numeral six."

(Continue to the end of the song.)

After the song has finished, discuss the concept of "line." Indicate to the students that the number line stopped at ten because the song stopped there, but it *could* go on and on to 100 or 1,000 or even 1,000,000 or more! "We don't have room on our paper, so we show just part of a line. The arrows at each end of the line show that the line goes on and on."

♪ Note the "action word" in each verse. Students could illustrate each verb by drawing it or by acting it out.

♪ Organize a skit in which nine students, each with a placard bearing a number from one to nine, act out the story while the others sing the song. The students watching can see the line become longer as each child joins it. After the climax when the teacher comes out to make ten, all the actors turn to face the audience in a living number line.

Order and the Number Line

Teaching Primary Math with Music © Dale Seymour Publications

Adding One
Makes the Numbers Grow

Waltz tempo

B♭   F7

If you start with one and you add one more, two is the an-swer, one
  start with five and you add one more, six is the an-swer, one

B♭   F7

more than be-fore. If you start with two and you add one more,
more than be-fore. If you start with six and you add one more,

Note to Teachers

This song and its converse, "The Numbers Get Smaller Each Time We Subtract" (page 14), help teach basic addition and subtraction facts.

When students learn a few facts, use just the song lyrics that are appropriate and then finish by singing the song's last line: "This is the song we sing to show that adding one makes the numbers grow."

♪ Class members can form a "living number line" to demonstrate addition. Each participating student should have a placard bearing a number from one to ten. As the song is sung, starting with "one," the first child comes up. As you "add one more" to make the next larger sum, the second child comes up and students can see that "one" and "one more" equals two. Continue until you reach ten. Conversely, with "The Numbers Get Smaller Each Time We Subtract" (page 14), each child leaves in order as the song progresses until only "one" remains.

♪ Showing subtraction right after you've shown addition on the "living number line" clearly demonstrates their relationship as the line grows longer or shorter.

then the new group has three._____ If you start with three and you
then the new group has seven._____ If you start with seven and you

add one more, four is the an-swer, one more than be-fore. If you
add one more, eight is the an-swer, one more than be-fore. If you

The Numbers Get Smaller Each Time We Subtract

Waltz tempo

G

If you start with ten and one goes a - way, Nine is the an - swer for
start with six and one goes a - way, Five is the an - swer for

D7 G C

nine will stay. If you start with nine and one goes a - way, The
five will stay. If you start with five and one goes a - way, The

Note to Teachers

This song, the converse of "Adding One Makes the Numbers Grow" (page 11), can be used to teach basic subtraction facts.

When students learn a few facts, use the appropriate lyrics of the song and then finish by singing the song's last line: "This we remember for it's a fact— the numbers get smaller each time we subtract."

♪ Class members can use a "living number line" to demonstrate subtraction. Start with ten students in a line, each with a placard bearing a number from one to ten. As the song progresses, beginning with "ten," each child leaves in order until only "one" remains.

Number Families

Note to Teachers

This song starts by stating that "Numbers have families, same as we do. They work and play together." Just like families, numbers can be hard work, but they can also be fun! "They have their very own rules" just as our families have rules. For example, one number family rule is "addend plus addend will give you a sum; subtract and you have a remainder."

"Number Families" teaches that for every one addition fact we know, we have a family of four! If we know 4 + 3 = 7, we also know 3 + 4 = 7, 7 − 3 = 4, and 7 − 4 = 3. This is one number family.

The first part of the song familiarizes students with beginning math vocabulary: *addend, sum, plus, subtract, remainder.*

The second part, "Think of a family 5 and 2, 5 and 2 is 7," can be used over and over with different number families that students suggest.

♪ You can make an *animal* number family for the bulletin board. The Teacher Sheet on page 19 has a blackline master for a family of turkeys. Photocopy them (enlarged) on colored paper and write the equations as shown.

Join sets to-geth-er or sep-a-rate sets, ad-di-tion or___ sub-trac-tion.___
if you have sev-en and take a-way 5,_____ what re-mains is 2._____ And

Ad-dend plus ad-dend will give you a sum; sub-tract and you have a re-main-der.___
if you have sev-en and take a-way 2,_____ then the re-main-der is 5._____

♪ For a math corner activity, photo-copy the animal number family paper dolls on page 20. Students paper clip the correct bibs on the animals.

♪ Demonstrate number families by using a "domino." Fold a rectangular piece of construction paper in half. Place colored circular stickers on it—for example, for the family 2, 3, and 5, the domino would look like this:

Hold it up and sing the second verse of the song as you demonstrate: "Think of a family 3 and 2. 3 and 2 is 5. Turn it around (do it) and what is the sum? 2 and 3 is 5. But if we have 5 and take away 3 (fold back the side with three stickers), what remains is 2. And if we have 5 and take away 2 (fold back the side with 2 stickers), then the remainder is 3." Students can make their own "dominoes" for practice.

Teaching Primary Math with Music © Dale Seymour Publications

Animal Number Families (1)

Example of a number family:

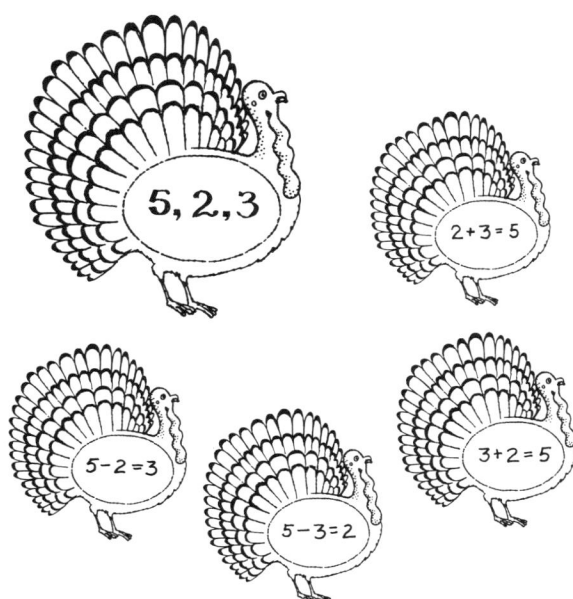

Animal Number Families (2)

You will need four copies of each smaller
animal and one copy of everything else.

4, 2, 6

2+4=6   6-2=4

4+2=6   6-4=2

5+2=7   7-5=2

5, 2, 7

2+5=7   7-2=5

9, 1, 10

9+1=10   10-9=1

1+9=10   10-1=9

Teaching Primary Math with Music © Dale Seymour Publications

If Zero's the Addend

Brightly

Look at the ad-dend.___ If ze-ro's its name, The sum and the o-ther ad-dend will be the same.

Note to Teachers

Sometimes understanding zero is a problem for students who are beginning addition. Here is a little song to help solve the problem—a cheerful reminder that zero doesn't ever add anything to the sum.

The Order of the Addends

Bouncy

Note to Teachers

This song explains the Commutative Rule, the order rule for addition. It tells us that the order in which we add the addends does not change the sum.

$$3 + 7 = 10$$

and

$$7 + 3 = 10$$

Therefore, if you know one of those facts, by turning the addends around you know *two* facts.

Similarly, the order of the *grouping* of the addends makes no difference:

$$2 + (3 + 5) = 2 + 8 = 10$$

and

$$(2 + 3) + 5 = 5 + 5 = 10$$

really very easy. It's a ball!___ The
or - der of the ad - dends does - n't mat - ter at all!___

♪ Introduce the concept of order by asking students these questions:

Is the order in which we do things always important?

Would you put your shoes on and then your socks? Would you take a bath and then undress?

If there are different foods on your dinner plate, does it matter which one you eat first or second or last? Would the result be the same?

Have students think of activities in which order does or does not matter.

Equivalent Sets

If there's a set of chil-dren and there's a set of pets, but
some of the chil-dren have-n't a-ny pets, the

Note to Teachers

The concept of equivalent sets is an important one. You can teach it as soon as order or the beginning addition facts are presented in the first grade. When multiplication is introduced, it can be defined as a short-cut for the addition of equivalent sets.

♪ Here is a method that quickly and graphically teaches about equivalent sets.

Teacher: "Everyone raise your right hand in a fist. Whenever I say, 'a man,' raise one finger." *(Do it with the students.)* "A man," (one finger), "a man," (one more finger), "a man" (third finger). "Keep them up."

"Now everyone raise your left fist. Whenever I say, 'a car,' raise a finger of your left fist. Everyone do it with me. A car," (one finger), "a car," (one more finger), "a car," (third finger).

"Put raised fingers of both hands together. Does each 'man' have a 'car'?" *(Students answer, "Yes.")*

"Here's the rule. If each one (one set) matches one (in the other set) the sets are *equivalent*. Are these sets equivalent?" *("Yes.")* "What would be the *number* of the set of men?" *("Three.")*

Teaching Primary Math with Music © Dale Seymour Publications

sets are NOT e-quiv-a-lents. They don't match one-for-one. *("Here's the rule"-spoken)* If

each one *("in one set")* match-es one *("in the other set")* the sets ARE e-quiv-a-lent.

"What is the *number* of the set of cars?" *("Three.")* "Do both sets have the *same number?"* *("Yes.")* "If the sets have the same number, they are equivalent sets."

"Let's try another. Right fists up! Whenever I say, 'a girl' this time, raise a finger of your right fist." *(Do it.)* "A girl," (one finger), "a girl," (second finger), "a girl," (third finger), "a girl," (fourth finger). "Keep them up. Raise your left fist. This time we'll see how many girls have books. Whenever I say, 'a book,' raise a finger from your left fist. A book," (first finger), "a book," (second finger), "a book," (third finger). "Look at your fingers."

"Does each girl have a book?" *(Students answer, "No.")* "Then does each one in one set match one in the other set?" *("No.")* "What would you have to do to make the sets equivalent?" *("Add a book.")*

"What is the *number* of the set of girls?" *(Students answer "Four.")* "What is the *number* of the set of books?" *("Three.")* "Do the sets have the same number?" *("No.")* "Then are these sets equivalent?" *("No.")*

"Now let's listen to a song about sets and see if you know whether they are equivalent or not ." *(Play the song. The sets in the song are not equivalent.)*

♪ You or the students can make up other verses of the song.

How Many Ways?

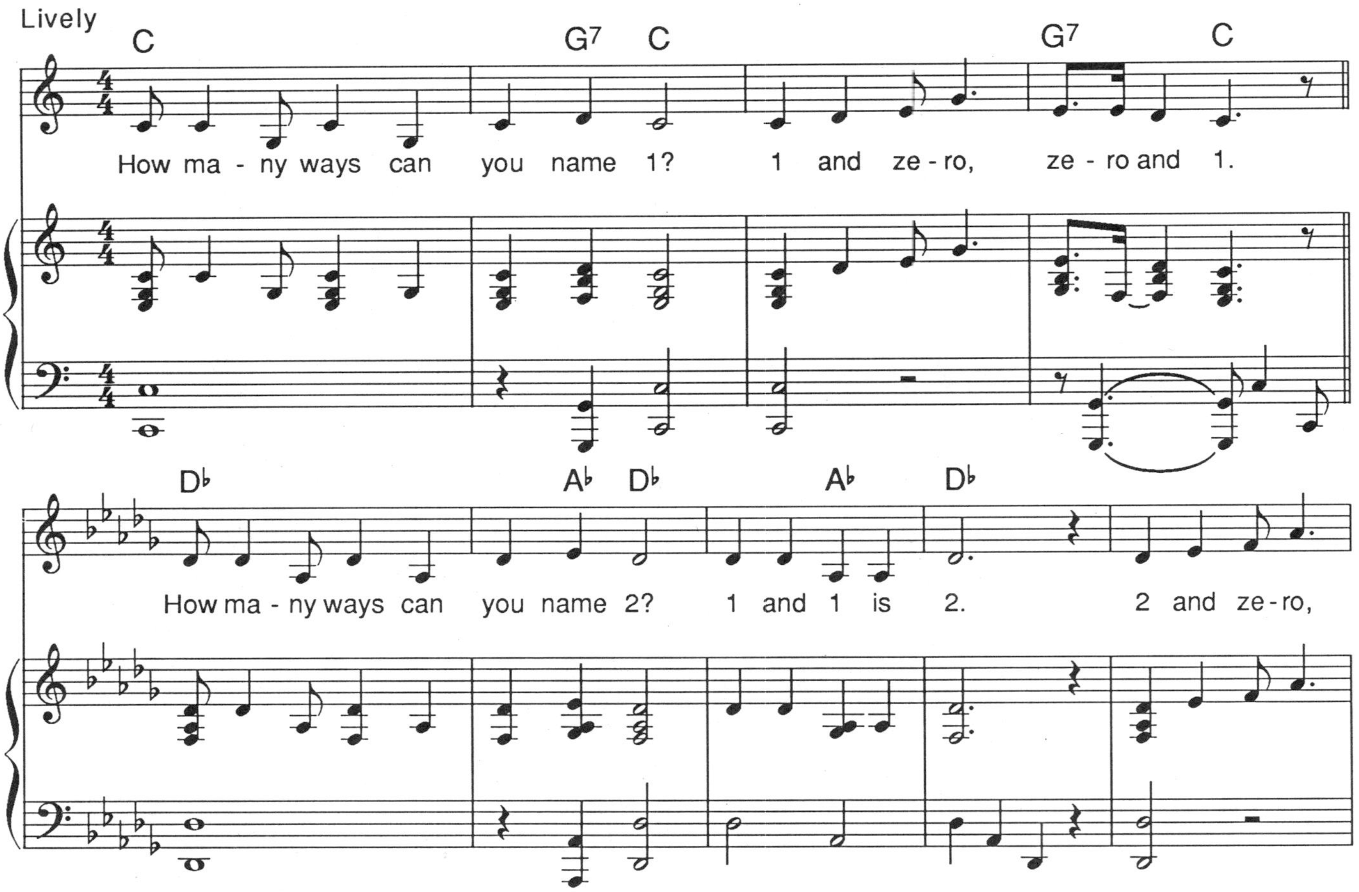

[Musical score: "Lively", key of C, with lyrics:]

How ma-ny ways can you name 1? 1 and ze-ro, ze-ro and 1.

[Second section, key of D♭:]

How ma-ny ways can you name 2? 1 and 1 is 2. 2 and ze-ro,

Note to Teachers

"How Many Ways?" is a proven method for reinforcing the sixty-five basic addition facts. The song's idea is to sing all the ways to name the sums from one to ten. The musical patterns reinforce the arithmetic patterns.

♪ Using the Student Worksheet on page 32, students make a number line "football" to answer the question "How many ways can you name 6?" Each student will draw an arc connecting each pair of numbers whose sum is 6. To reinforce the facts in making the "football" the child writes them vertically so that the pattern is evident. The "football" will look like the example at right.

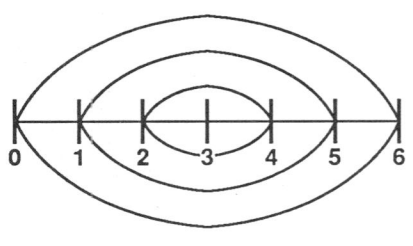

♪ Have students complete the *Sixty-five Facts* Student Worksheet (page 33) for extra practice. Circle the equations in the table that students need to practice (as a class or individually) and write two of them on the blank lines. You might send this sheet home with students.

Think of the moment just before dismissal, when all the students are in line, ready and eager for the bell—but waiting. Use the moment to have students sing, "How many ways can you name 7?" (8, 10, or any number they've been working on) for a happy and useful ending to the day.

1 and 4 is 5.　3 and 2 is 5.　2 and 3 is 5.　5 and ze-ro,

ze-ro and 5.　How ma-ny ways can you name 6?　5 and 1 is 6.

1 and 5 is 6.　4 and 2 is 6.　2 and 4 is 6.　3 and 3 is 6.

6 and ze-ro, ze-ro and 6.　How ma-ny ways can you name 7?

Number Line Football

How many ways can you name 6?

6+0

5+1

4+2

3+3

2+4

1+5

0+6

Make a football showing the ways to name 10.

How many ways can you name 10?

```
├───┼───┼───┼───┼───┼───┼───┼───┼───┼───┤
0   1   2   3   4   5   6   7   8   9   10
```

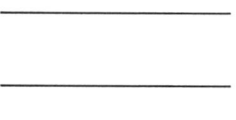

Sixty-five Facts

How many ways can you name...

1	2	3	4	5	6	7	8	9	10
1+0	2+0	3+0	4+0	5+0	6+0	7+0	8+0	9+0	10+0
0+1	1+1	2+1	3+1	4+1	5+1	6+1	7+1	8+1	9+1
	0+2	1+2	2+2	3+2	4+2	5+2	6+2	7+2	8+2
		0+3	1+3	2+3	3+3	4+3	5+3	6+3	7+3
			0+4	1+4	2+4	3+4	4+4	5+4	6+4
				0+5	1+5	2+5	3+5	4+5	5+5
					0+6	1+6	2+6	3+6	4+6
						0+7	1+7	2+7	3+7
							0+8	1+8	2+8
								0+9	1+9
									0+10

Make a number football of these equations:

_____

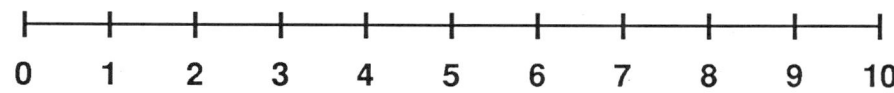

_____

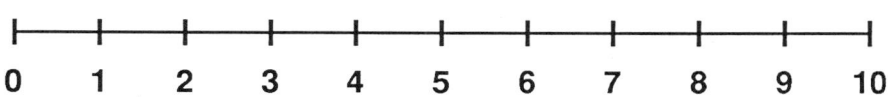

Teaching Primary Math with Music © Dale Seymour Publications

Five Steps to Problem Solving

Slowly

What do you want to know?

What are the sets? What must you do with them?

Note to Teachers

There are almost as many differently phrased "steps for problem solving" as there are books written about the subject. One series simply states, "Read the problem. Decide what to do. Find the answer." This is too simplistic. Read the problem? Sure. But first the student must ask, "What do I want to know?" Then, "What are the facts or sets? What must I do with them? Join them (addition), or separate them—take some away (subtraction)? Maybe compare them (subtraction again)?" In the early primary grades the only computational skills students have are addition and subtraction, so much early problem solving deals with putting together and taking away.

Having decided on the appropriate action, "Write the equation with a plus or a minus sign" and "Solve the equation" to find out "what you wanted to know."

Teaching Primary Math with Music © Dale Seymour Publications

Dm   A7   Dm

Join them or sep-a-rate them May-be com-pare. Write the e-qua-tion with a

G   Dm   A7   Dm

plus or a mi-nus sign. Solve the e-qua-tion. That's what you want-ed to know.___

Oh, We Only Have Ten Digits

Note to Teachers

Place value is a very important concept. The song "Oh, We Only Have Ten Digits" is one way to make it interesting.

♪ Before singing the song you can tell the following story, which condenses the history of our numerical system into a few moments. You can illustrate the numbers on the blackboard or overhead projector as the story unfolds.

A long, long time ago when people didn't have any numerals, they used to count on their fingers. When they needed to count more than ten, they used their toes. But when twenty wasn't enough, someone who was very smart said, "Let's make pictures to represent numbers." Different groups of people made different pictures to represent numbers. After a long time, some people made a line that looked like the finger they had used for counting, and it looked like our numeral 1. *(Write "1.")* Then they made a picture to show *two* things. It looked like our numeral 2. *(Write "2.")* Eventually, the picture for three things came to look like our numeral 3. Then came 4, 5, 6, 7, 8, 9 *(write the numbers)*, and the people said "Stop! If we keep making more of these pictures, we will never be able to remember them all!"

Teaching Primary Math with Music © Dale Seymour Publications

But one person who was very smart said, "We have to have one more. We need a picture to show when we have *no* things." So they made one more picture, called zero. They called the ten pictures "digits," the word they had used long ago for "fingers"—which they had used to count with.

"But how can we show big numbers with only these ten digits?" someone asked. After thinking for quite a long time, they decided that all they needed were these ten digits—if they had special places in which to put them. The places would have special values. That is why we call the method they invented *place value.*

♪ To illustrate place value, you can use links of a chain (plastic link toys or paper clips.) Hold up one link to represent the digit 1, and write it on the blackboard. Ten links joined together show that this is also 1—one group of ten. But to show that it isn't just one link, that digit has to go in a different place, the tens' place. Use a group of one hundred links to show the hundreds' place in the same way.

Tens and Ones Pockets

To use the Tens and Ones Pockets, you will need: ❶ pockets and ❷ cards. Use the pockets with students to show the sum or remainder in addition or subtraction problems. This is useful for quick drill, checking individual students, and reinforcing the concept of place value.

pockets:

1. Draw a rectangle measuring 18" x 6". Mark it and fold it as shown. One sheet of 12" x 18" colored construction paper makes two sets of pockets.

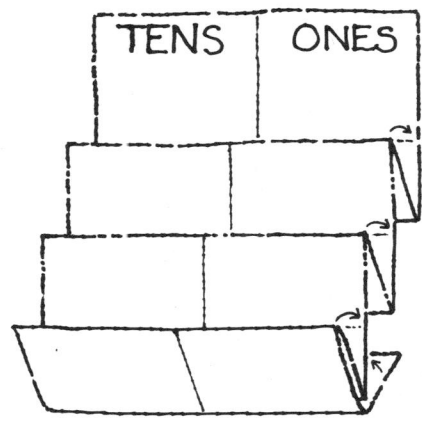

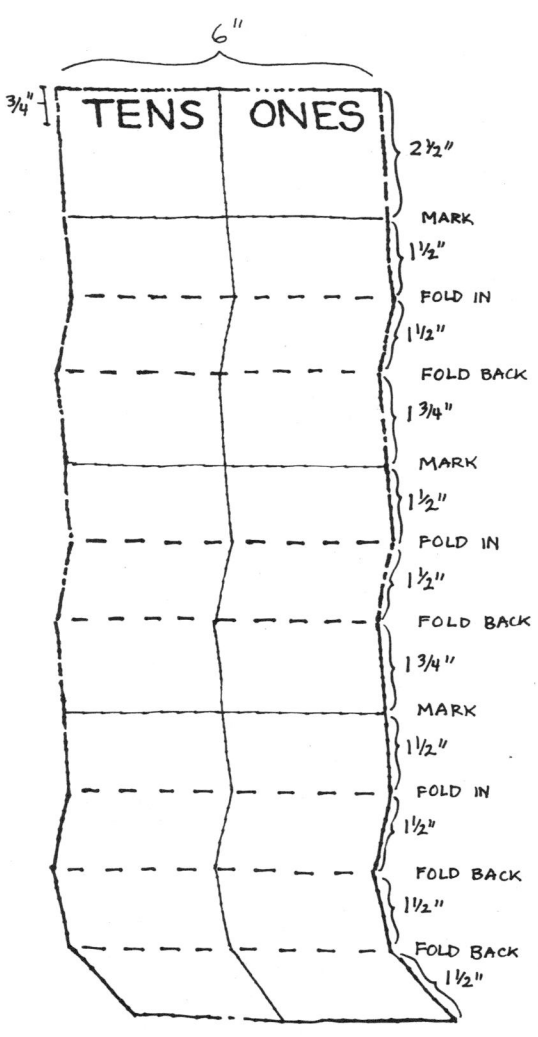

After folding it, staple the sides closed. The finished pockets will look like this:

cards:

Cut out two sets of 2 1/4" x 3" cards from tagboard, numbered from 0–9. Make sure to write the number on the *top* half of the card only, so it will be visible when the card is in the pocket.

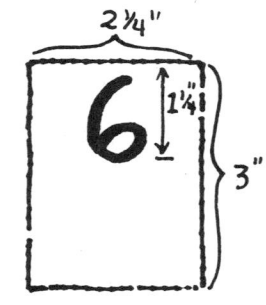

Hundreds, Tens, and Ones Pockets

To use the Hundreds, Tens, and Ones Pockets, you will need:

❶ pockets, made from an 18" x 3 1/2" strip of colored construction paper.

❷ tagboard cards, including one for each of the ten digits, two cards with plus signs, and one card each for "hundreds," "tens," and "ones."

Make the pockets from the strip of paper as shown.

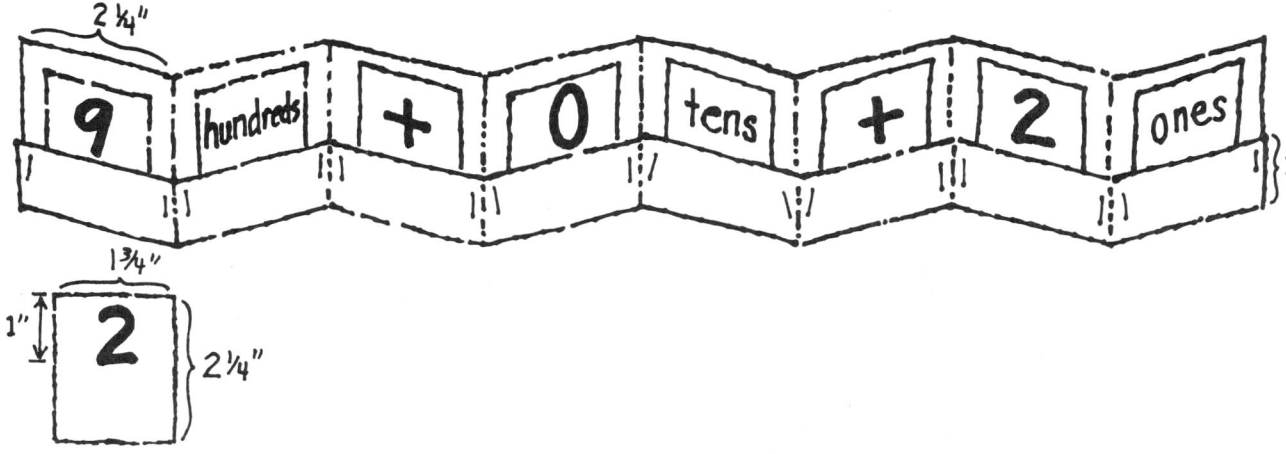

Turn up and staple the bottom inch of paper to form pockets. Score eight 2 1/4" sections so they will bend. You can fold the sections to show as much as you like:

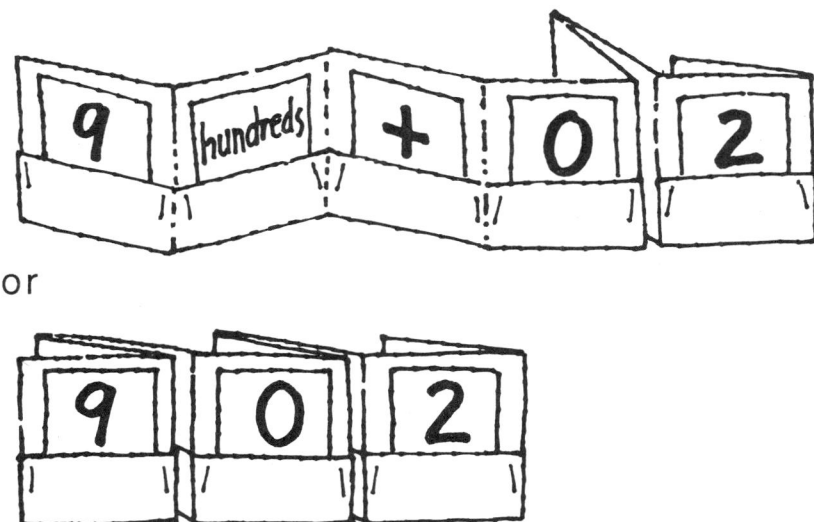

or

This tool is useful for place-value drill and for graphically showing expanded notation.

Twenty-six Apples

Moderately fast

Twen - ty six ap - ples hang - ing on a tree. Thir - ty eight ap - ples

on an - oth - er tree. Put them to - geth - er. "How ma - ny in all?"____ means

Note to Teachers

"Twenty-six Apples" is actually a problem in addition-with-regrouping (or "carrying," although nothing is really carried) with the algorithm put to music.

Use the phrases in the lyrics to teach the algorithm before you use the song.

"Tens in the ones' place just won't do!" (the crux of the matter) can be illustrated by showing that when 38, for instance, is added to 26, "add the ones, then the tens. That's the thing to do." The sum of 8 + 6, 14, has two digits; one ten and four ones. Therefore, the four ones must be put in the ones' place and the one ten must be put in its proper place—"in the tens' place above the line"—and be careful, "don't leave that brand new ten behind!"

$$
\begin{array}{r}
1 \\
3\,8 \\
+\ 2\,6 \\
\hline
\textcircled{6}\,4
\end{array}
$$

You can change the numbers and situation of the song to fit other problems. Children can make up problems and the class can sing them—for example, "Seventeen children sliding down the hill, twenty-nine children climbing up the hill. Put them together," and so forth.

Long after the lessons for addition-with-regrouping have been taught, the song can be used to cheerfully reinforce this skill.

thing to do. Then add all the ones. If they're more than nine, put the

tens in the tens' place a - bove the line. Now add all the tens and your

an - swer you'll find, but don't leave the brand new ten be - hind!

Twen - ty six ap - ples hang - ing on a tree. Thir - ty eight ap - ples

on an-oth-er tree. We did the ad-di-tion. Now what is the sum? Six-ty four is our an-swer, and we're all done!

When We Subtract

Lively waltz tempo

When we sub-tract, "How ma-ny are left?" is the thing we want to know. What we

start with goes on top. What we take a-way goes be-low. If we
five goes on the top. Twen-ty nine___ goes down be-low. If we

Note to Teachers

A song about subtraction with regrouping might seem a bit strange, but here it is—with the complete algorithm built in!

Young students love to sing the song's ending, "it's as easy as apple pie," but, of course, it really isn't. Before singing the song, they will need a great deal of practice in regrouping a two-digit number into tens and ones and representing the regrouping process.

Children can happily practice regrouping by changing the numbers in the second verse and solving the new problems. Singing the songs will be their reward—and extra reinforcement!

♪ See the Teacher Sheet on page 47 for a fun and effective lesson in subtraction with regrouping.

Subtraction with Regrouping

One way to help children see how regrouping works is to act it out. If you have 35 students, for example, have them form three groups of ten. Put masking tape around each group of ten to define it as one set of ten.

Then break the tape of the last group of ten and let the children from that group join with the five ones. Now the number 35 has been regrouped into two groups of ten and fifteen ones.

Multiplication and Division

Moderately

Take the num - ber of sets, e - quiv - a - lent sets, times the
But,___ take a - way sets, e - quiv - a - lent sets, from the

num - ber of mem - bers with - in one._____ That's
num - ber of things all to - geth - er,_____ And

Note to Teachers

Multiplication can be explained as a short-cut for the addition of equivalent sets. When introducing it that way, display several equivalent sets on the blackboard. If students do not know about equivalent sets, teach them in just a few minutes by using the technique given with the song "Equivalent Sets" on page 24.

♪ To explain multiplication, write on the blackboard:

$$(x\ x)\ (x\ x)\ (x\ x)\ (x\ x)\ (x\ x)\ (x\ x)$$

Ask for the number of items in each set, and then write it under each set:

$$(x\ x)\ (x\ x)\ (x\ x)\ (x\ x)\ (x\ x)\ (x\ x)$$
$$2 \qquad 2 \qquad 2 \qquad 2 \qquad 2 \qquad 2$$

Teacher: "Do the sets all have the same number?" *(Students answer, "Yes.")* "Are they equivalent sets?" *("Yes.")* "What sign must we put between each number to show that we will add?"*("The plus sign.")* *(Add the plus sign.)*

"Let's read it '2 plus 2 plus 2 plus 2 plus 2 plus 2.' What is the answer?" *("Twelve.")* *(Write the answer on the board.)*

D⁷

mul - ti - pli - ca - tion. It's eas - y to do. You'll
you'll have di - vi - sion, what ev - er the time What -

D⁷   G

find it's fun when you be - gin one._____
ev - er the place or the weath - er._____

"That's a long way to find the answer. Let's count by twos to see what the answer will be." *(Count 2, 4, 6, 8, 10, 12.)* "That's a little better. But an even shorter way is to 'Take the number of sets'— 6" *(write "6")* "'equivalent sets—times *(write the times sign)* the number of members within one.' How many members in one of the sets?" *("Two.")* "Six times two equals twelve. 'That's multiplication. It's easy to do. You'll find it's fun when you begin one.' "*(Sing the first verse of the song.)*

You can also explain the concept with the number line:

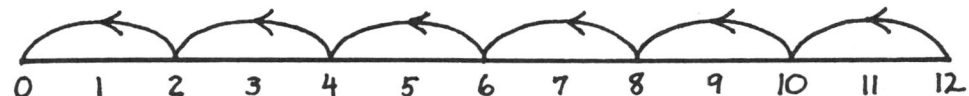

♪ Division is the opposite or converse of multiplication, so this technique will work backwards:

Teacher: "This time we know how many things there are all together— 12—so let's take away sets of 2, equivalent sets:

12 − 2 = 10	10 − 2 = 8	8 − 2 = 6
6 − 2 = 4	4 − 2 = 2	2 − 2 = 0

How many sets of 2 did we take away to reach zero? Count them. *("Six.")* So we can say that 12 can be divided into sets of 2 six times, or 12 ÷ 2 = 6." *(Sing the second verse of the song.)*

♪ Use the *Multiplication and Division* Student Worksheet on page 50 to reinforce the concepts.

Multiplication and Division

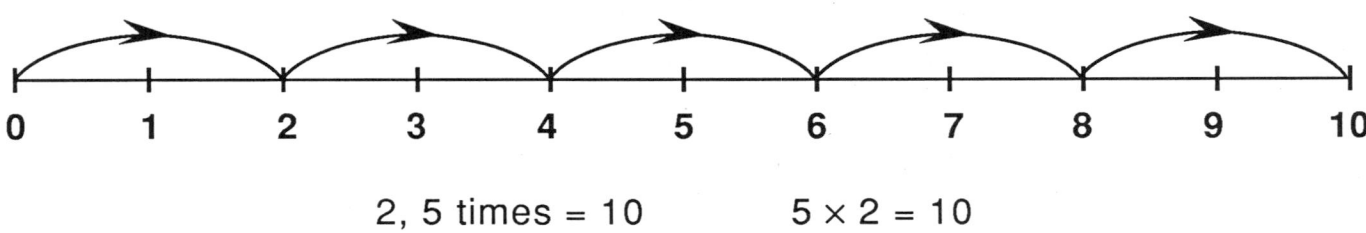

2, 5 times = 10   5 × 2 = 10

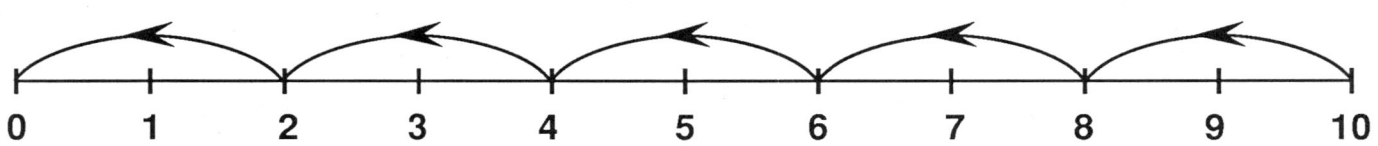

Sets of 2 can be taken from 10, 5 times.

10 ÷ 2 = 5

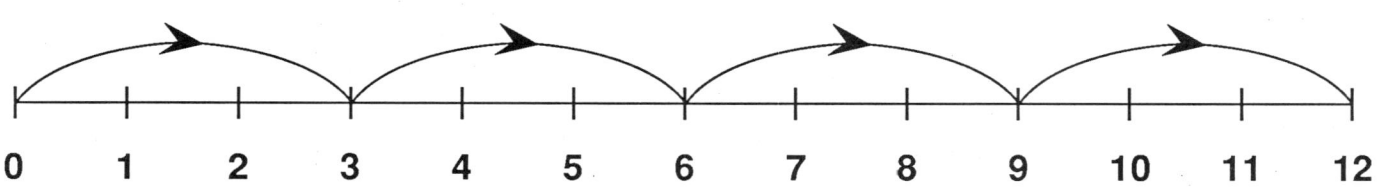

Write the equation: _____ × _____ = 12

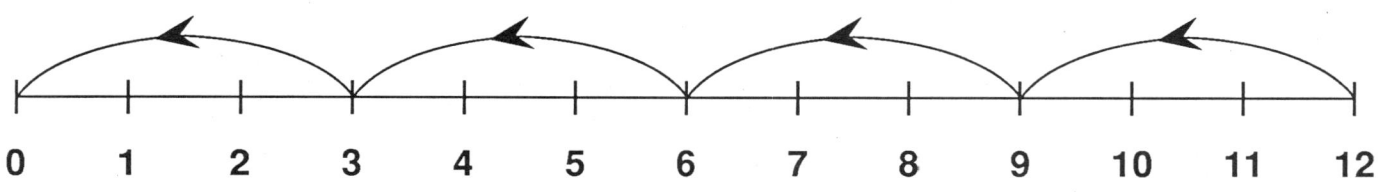

Write the equation: 12 ÷ _____ = _____

A Better Way

Note to Teachers

This song explains the material in "Multiplication and Division" (page 48) in a different way, and includes a bit of skip-counting.

too much time, takes up too much space. To

count by twos, threes or fives is O. K. but to

mul - ti - ply is a bet - ter way! So

The Clock Measures Time

Fairly lively

The ther - mom - e - ter meas - ures the___ cold and the heat. A___
We get up in the morn - ing. We have break - fast at eight. We___
Then it's back to our work, for there's___ so much to learn. While we

scale meas - ures things that we buy or we eat. A___
hur - ry to school so that we won't be late. The___
work both the clock - hands con - tin - ue to turn. We go

Note to Teachers

This song and the next two songs, "The Clock" and "On the Clock Face Number Line," are a trilogy of songs about time.

"The Clock Measures Time" explains that the clock is one of many measuring devices, such as the thermometer, the scale, and the ruler, and "with minutes and hours, the clock measures time." It tells what we do throughout the day as the clock hands keep turning, "even while we're asleep."

♪ Students can illustrate booklets of their activities throughout the day.

♪ They can make a "time line" mural of their daily activities to post on their wall at home. This is good practice in developing sequence.

♪ They can act out what they do at different times of the day. Accompany each activity with an illustration of a clock showing the appropriate time.

♪ With older students, organize a science activity in which they look up other devices for measuring such as the speedometer, tape measure,

Teaching Primary Math with Music © Dale Seymour Publications

ru - ler helps meas - ure a ___ part of a line, And with
clock - hands keep mov - ing. They ___ tell us that soon, We'll be
home, have our sup - per. In - to bed we will creep, And the

min - utes and hou - rs a clock meas - ures time.
eat - ing, for lunch - time will come a - round noon.
clock meas - ures time e - ven while we're a - sleep.

7:30 a.m.   8:00 a.m.   a.m.
MY DAY

odometer, pressure gauge, cooking timer, anemometer, trundle wheel, and others. You can make a mural featuring the song lyrics and illustrations of these different instruments. For enrichment, students could also research and study gears and machines.

The Clock

Moderately

The clock face is a num-ber line. In-stead of straight it's round. It
Straight up, a-round, straight up a-gain, One hour that min-ute hand sweeps. While

mea-sures_hours_ from one to twelve. No o-thers may be found. Each
just to the ve-ry next nu-mer-al, the slow-er hour hand creeps. That

Note to Teachers

"The Clock" reviews the parts of the clock face, showing that it is a round number line. The song tells how the hands work and explains how to tell time to the hour and the half-hour—generally part of the first-grade curriculum. You can use the song to introduce, summarize, or review the material.

♪ You may want to demonstrate with a clock. One with gears clearly shows how the minute hand completes a full circle as the hour hand only "creeps" to the next numeral. This is more accurate than a cardboard demonstration clock, and students can see the gears work as the hands move.

♪ After the lesson, while the song is being played or sung, students can take turns acting as the "teacher" by moving the clock hands on the toy clock to act out the words in the song.

On the Clock Face
Number Line

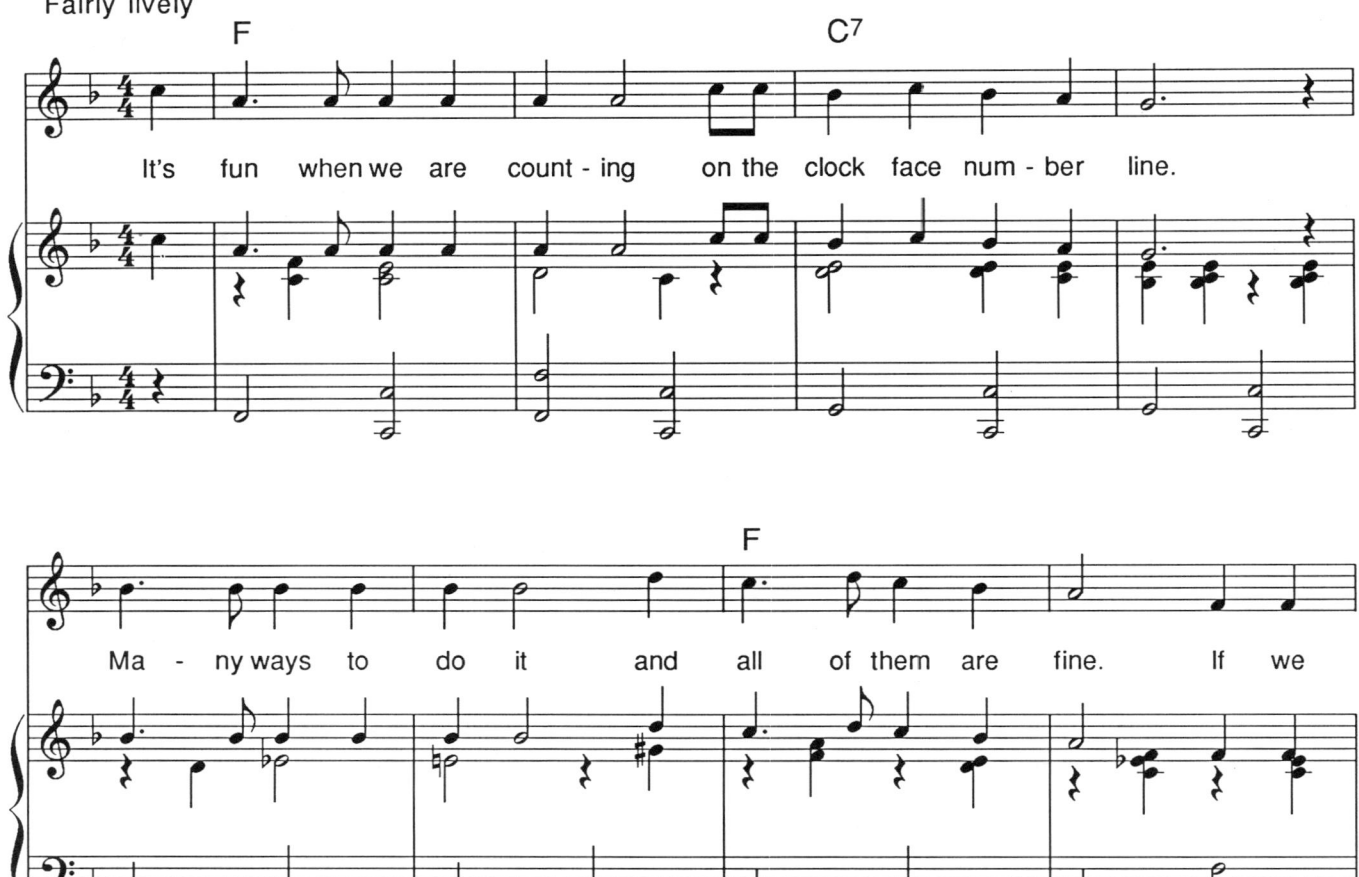

Fairly lively

It's fun when we are count-ing on the clock face num-ber line.

Ma - ny ways to do it and all of them are fine. If we

Note to Teachers

"On the Clock Face Number Line" tells about many ways to count around the clock—by the hour, from one to twelve; by the minute, from one to sixty; by five minute intervals; and by quarter hours.

♪ You can count the hours around the clock two times, a.m. and p.m., to equal twenty-four hours, one day. You can also introduce seconds if the students can count to sixty. For gifted groups, you might introduce clock arithmetic—counting forward or backward on the clock (for example, $11 + 3 = 2$, $8 + 5 = 1$, $4 - 5 = 11$.)

Teaching Primary Math with Music © Dale Seymour Publications

Twen - ty, twen-ty-five, thir - ty, Straight down, we say "half - past." Then it's

thir-ty five, for - ty, for-ty-five.__ That's "qua - ter to,"__ and then It's

fif - ty, fif-ty-five six - ty. Straight up! "O' - clock" a - gain!

How Many Pennies Will Match a Dime?

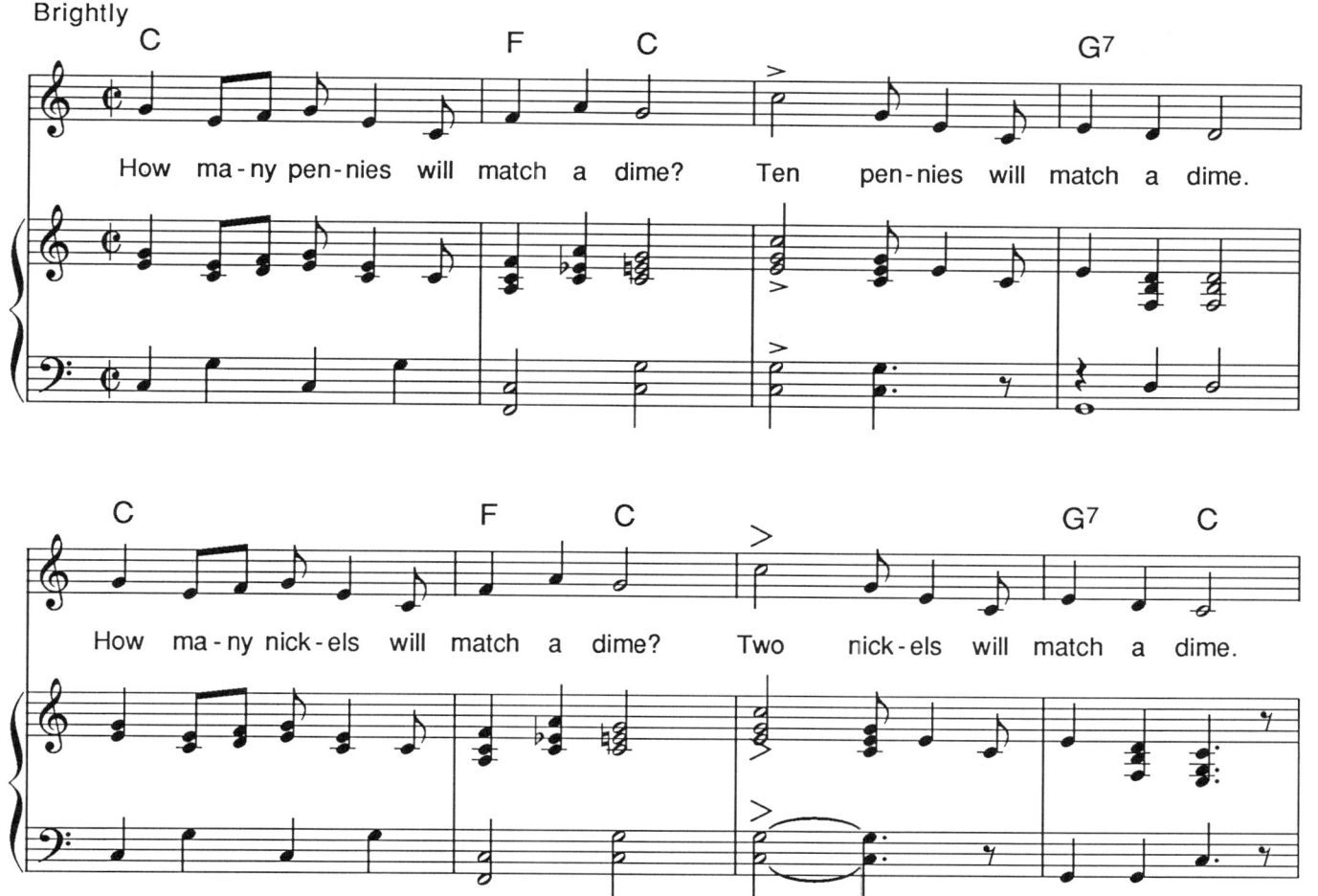

Note to Teachers

This song and the next two songs are about money.

Sometimes we assume that students come to us with skills that they actually do not have. One day, getting ready to play a trading game with a group of first-graders, I asked a little girl, "How many pennies make a nickel?" Her wide-eyed answer—"I dunno"—inspired me to write "How Many Pennies Will Match a Dime?" The song deals only with pennies, nickels, and dimes. One first-grade group sang the song over and over while walking to a nearby bank!

♪ The class can be divided into two parts. For a related language arts activity using choral speaking, have one side of the room speak or sing the question and the other side, the answer.

Is there a-ny o-ther way to do it? Yes there is, — and I'm sure you knew it.

Ten pen-nies or two nick-els will do. Five pen-nies and a nick-el will, too.
One nick-el and five pen-nies will, too.

Teaching Primary Math with Music © Dale Seymour Publications

Coins

Note to Teachers

This song explains why we need to know about coins. It covers the different coins that add up to a nickel, a dime, and a quarter, and the fact that dimes are tens and pennies are ones. It includes practice in skip-counting and explains how to use place value when writing the numerals.

"Coins" has been especially successful with third grade.

count to five— a nick-el is just the same.

You can change five pen-nies for a nick-el in a-ny trad-ing

game. Start with a pen-ny and count to ten; ten

Teaching Primary Math with Music © Dale Seymour Publications

Five Pennies Make a Nickel

Note to Teachers

It's always good to have a corner where students may go for special activities when their other work is finished. One of my favorite activities for a math corner is "Make a Dollar."

♪ All the component parts are contained in a zipper-lock plastic bag. They include a construction-paper game board and 34 tagboard pieces representing quarters, dimes, and nickels, to match the spaces on the board. Photocopy the blackline masters on pages 69 and 70 onto heavyweight paper or colored paper that can be glued to tagboard. (See next page for instructions.)

twen - ty nick - els, one hun - dred pen - nies will do it, too.

To use "Make a Dollar," the student covers the board with puzzle pieces to make a dollar—for example, three 25-cent pieces, two 10-cent pieces, and one 5-cent piece. If necessary, use the words of this song to get started. The student then writes down how he or she did it, mixes up the pieces, and "makes a dollar" another way. There are twenty-nine ways to "make a dollar." Perhaps an enterprising child who discovers a pattern can make a list. Fitting the puzzle pieces together is an incentive for students—they love to work with it.

♪ Younger students can play "Make a Quarter" with one-, five-, and ten-cent pieces (pages 71 and 72).

Make a Dollar (1)

Make a Dollar (2)

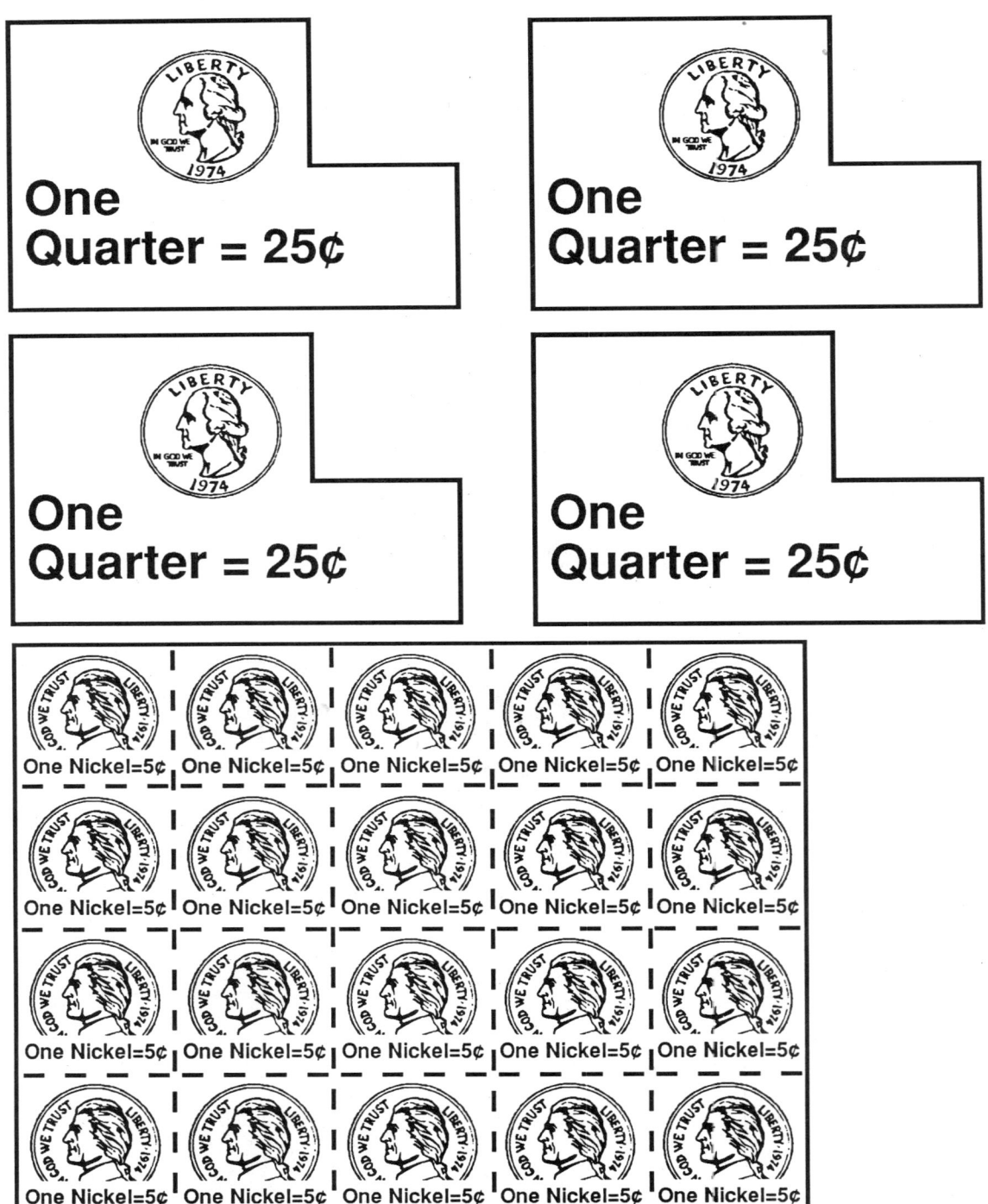

Make a Quarter (1)

One Dime = 10¢

One Dime = 10¢

Make a Quarter (2)

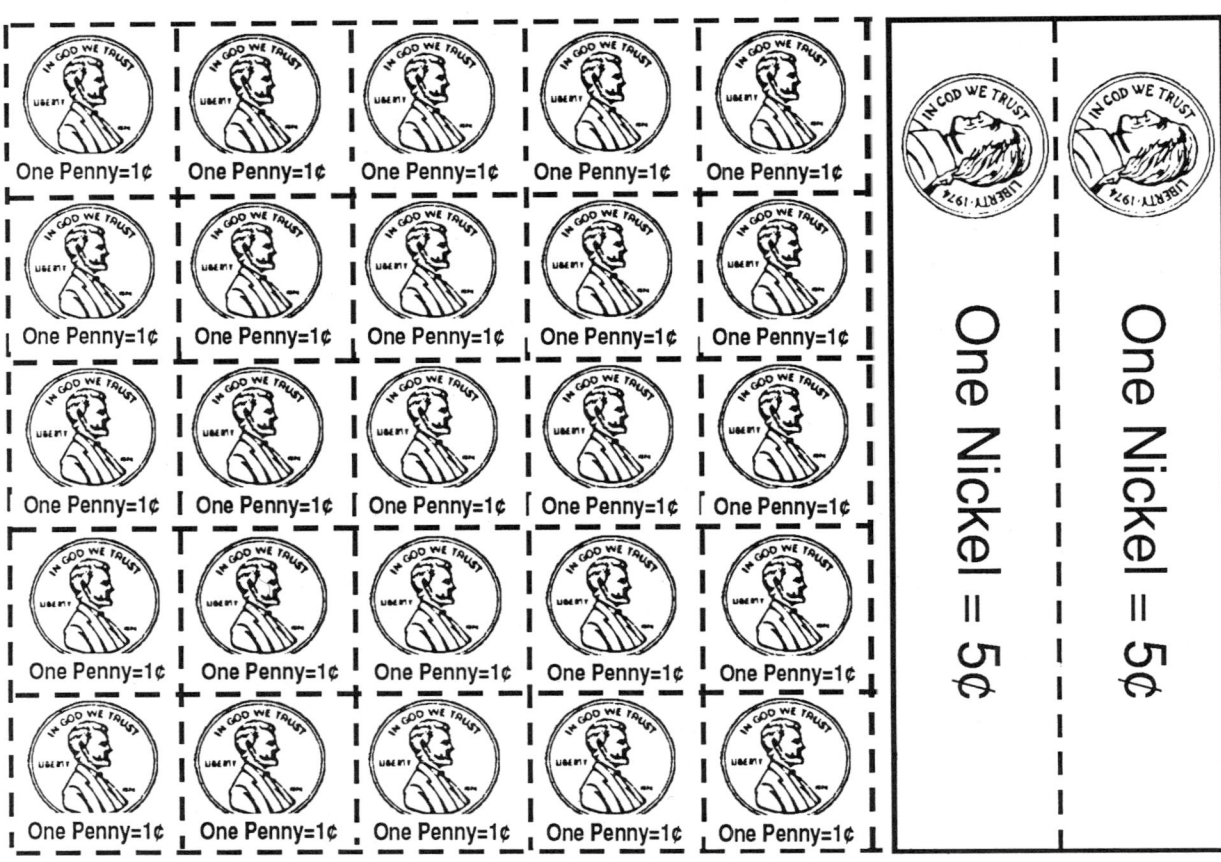

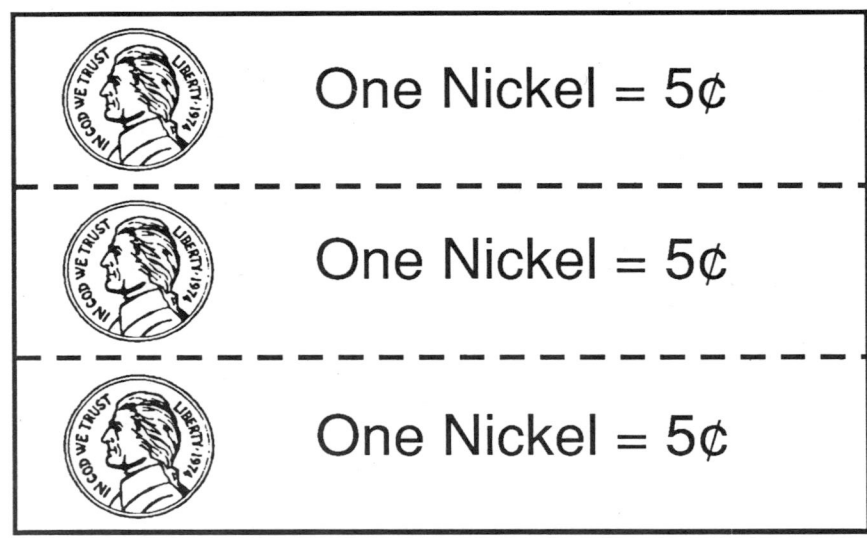

    Teaching Primary Math with Music © Dale Seymour Publications

Shapes

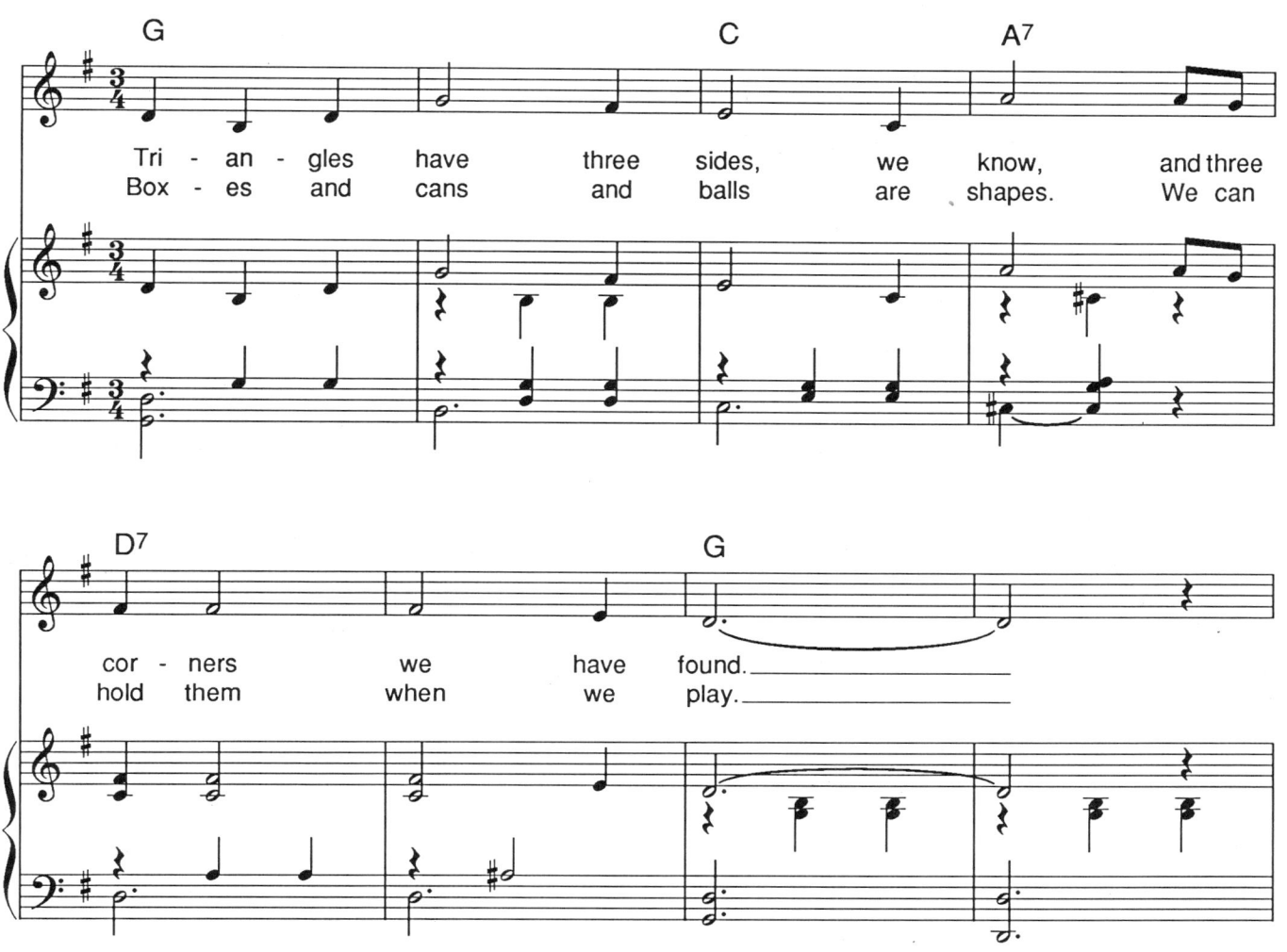

Note to Teachers

"Shapes" is a beginning geometry song. The first verse tells about flat shapes, while the second verse introduces three-dimensional figures—"we can hold them when we play."

Discussing "boxes and cans and balls" will lead students to realize that not all shapes are flat, as they see them in posters, on walls, or in textbooks.

♪ Students may look for objects in the room that are examples of various shapes, such as doors, windows, clocks, boxes, coins, or globes.

♪ Students can make individual booklets in the shape being studied. They can draw objects or paste magazine pictures of objects with that shape on the pages of their booklets. If their abilities warrant, students may label their illustrations. You might want to have students sing "Shapes" while they are working on their booklets. You can use the finished booklets to decorate a bulletin board.

Squares have four sides. They're all the same. But a
We can roll a can or a ball, But with

cir - cle goes round and round.
cor - ners a box will stay.

A Curve Is a Path

Lively

A curve is a path. It goes from place to place, con-

nect-ing ma-ny, ma-ny points through all of space.

1. Some curves are closed curves and
2. Some curves are straight curves, they're

Note to Teachers

This is a beginning geometry song.

Asked to name the tiniest thing they can think of, students will find it hard to think of something tinier than an ant! Suggest that they think of the tip of a sharpened pencil or the end of a needle to describe a point. We represent it by a dot, and we name it with a capital letter—for example, point A.

The idea of a *curve* as a set of points connected to make a path is a very basic geometric concept. However, it is difficult for children to conceptualize. You might bring the concept within students' experience by talking about the path they take from their house to school, or their room to the principal's office, as a set of points connected to become a path or curve.

F		G⁷		C		G aug

some are not.__ The shapes they make may dif-fer quite__ a lot.__ A

lines you know.__ A line seg-ment stops but a line will just go.__

cir-cle goes round, and round, and round. In a

Curves can be many different *shapes*. A curve that starts at one point and ends at that same point is a *closed curve*. A circle is a closed curve. A curve that starts at one point and ends somewhere else is an *open curve*. The letter U is an open curve. A *line* is a *straight curve* that keeps on going in both directions. The "line" we make with a ruler is only a part of a line—a *line segment*—that begins and ends at certain points.

♪ To make an attractive bulletin board about these geometric concepts, you will need construction paper, glue, and black yarn. Yellow paper with black yarn is very colorful. Squeeze out glue onto colored paper in the shapes that you want. Cover them with pieces of yarn and label them. That's all!

tri - an - gle three sides are found. A square is a rec - tan - gle

but BE - WARE! Ev - er - y rec - tan - gle is - n't a square!

A Circle

Note to Teachers

After teaching a lesson with several new words and concepts, it is always refreshing to have a review already prepared for you, one that will keep the students happy while reviewing and reinforcing the material. This song is such a review. It names and defines the parts of the circle. If you play the song on tape, you can point out facts mentioned in the song, such as "the length of every radius in a circle's the same," or check on students' work while they are singing the song.

circle again,___ that line segment's a diameter. And then, the length of a diameter's a radius times two! If you sing this song another time you'll have a review.___ A circle!

A Measurement Song

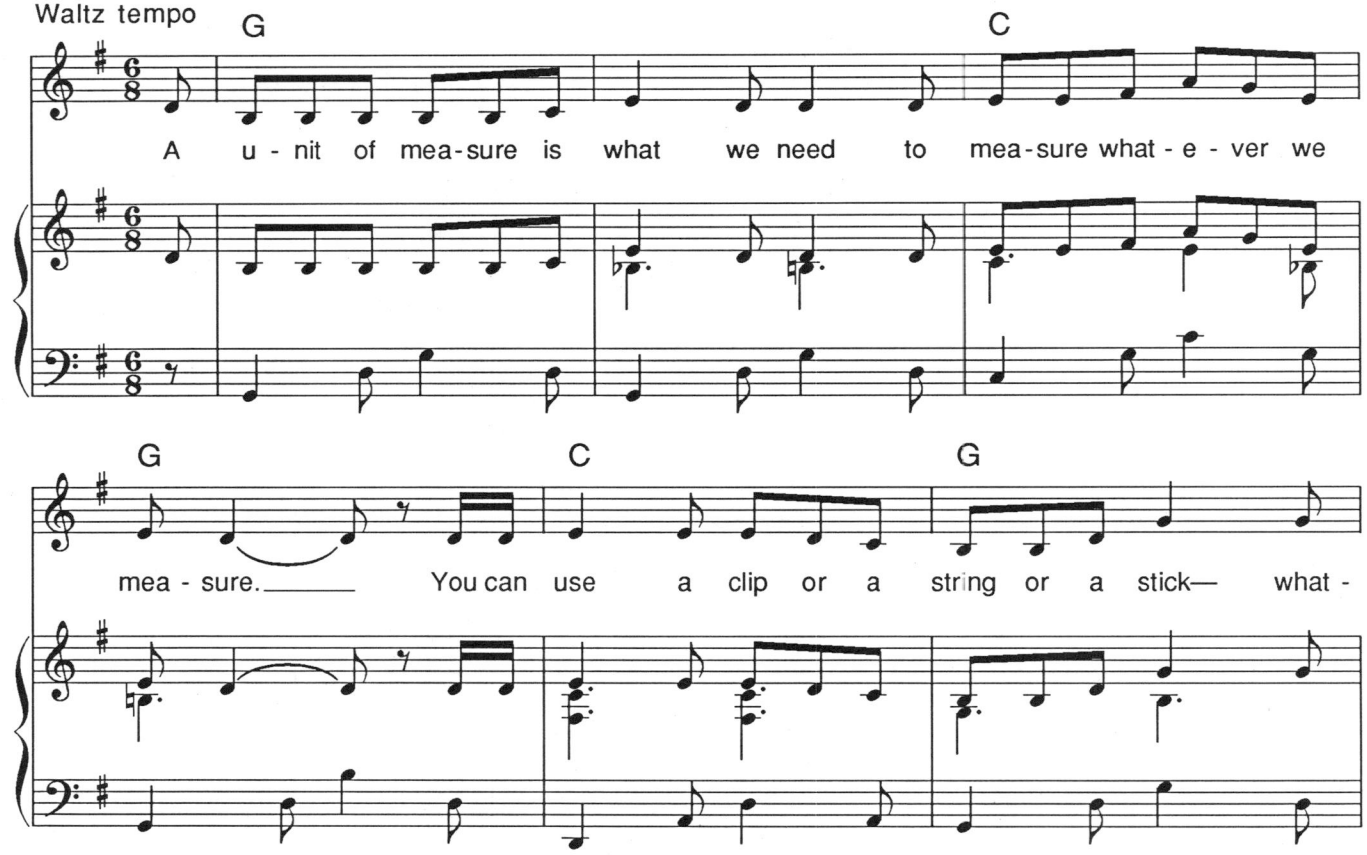

Note to Teachers

The very first line of "A Measurement Song"—"A unit of measure is what we need to measure whatever we measure."—is the essence of all measurement. Using hands-on activities to help students understand the need for a standard unit of measure can be very interesting. Asking students how many hands, thumbs, and paperclips wide their desks are will teach them that different units used to measure an object will result in different measurements. Comparing measurements using different units will teach students that they must count the number of times the unit is used and then name the unit to arrive at the measurement. The number is the measure—six—but the number and the named unit is the measurement—six inches.

♪ The story of the king who asked a carpenter to build a bed for his queen illustrates the need for standard units.

The king measured how long and how wide the bed would have to be with his foot. "It must be four feet by five feet," he told the carpenter. After a week the carpenter came back and proudly presented the bed to the king. But when the queen tried it, it was much too small. The carpenter had measured the correct number of feet, but he had measured using *his* feet, which were much smaller than the king's feet!

e - ver is your plea-sure._____ Just count and then name the

u - nits you use, but to make it much sim - pler and nea - ter,_____ we'll all

have the same mea-sure and mea-sure-ment, too, us-ing inch or cen-ti-me-ter.___

After that, the king decided on a standard length to be called a "foot." Other standard measures came to be: large units like a yard or a mile, and small units like an inch or centimeter.

♪ Working in groups of two, students can measure each other's height, arms, feet, waist, and head using rulers, tape measures, yardsticks or metersticks. You might have students estimate before they measure and compare their guesses to the correct measurements. They can put their results in a table. Ask questions such as "Who is taller? How much taller?", "Who is shorter?", "Who weighs more?", or "Whose arm is longer?" The table can be extended to include the entire class.

A Centimeter Measurement Song

Choose a pen - cil, string or fin - ger when you mea - sure.

Count the u - nits and be sure to say their

Note to Teachers

"A Centimeter Measurement Song" suggests using the centimeter, the metric unit of length. "A Measurement Song" (page 80) uses the inch *or* centimeter. Both songs stress that a standard unit is necessary for measurement. And it's fun to sing about it!

♪ Students will have fun playing the *Centimeter Crawl* game—and learn to measure the centimeter, too! You will need:

• a gameboard of tagboard or construction paper. You can photocopy the blackline master on page 86, or copy it in a larger size.

• a deck of game cards. Photocopy page 87 on colored paper and cut out the cards.

• differently-colored buttons or other small objects to use as counters (one per player)

• a centimeter ruler

name._____ But if we all use dif - ferent

u - nits when we mea-sure,_____ then our

Two to four students can play. To play the game, each player draws a card from the deck, which is face down. To move, the player follows the directions on the card, such as "Go ahead the number of centimeters in line segment A." The player puts the card face down in a pile of discarded cards and then must measure the designated line segment to find the number of spaces to move. Each "happy" space moves a player forward three spaces, while each "sad" space sends a player back three spaces. The player who reaches the centipede's head first wins.

The Centimeter Crawl (1)

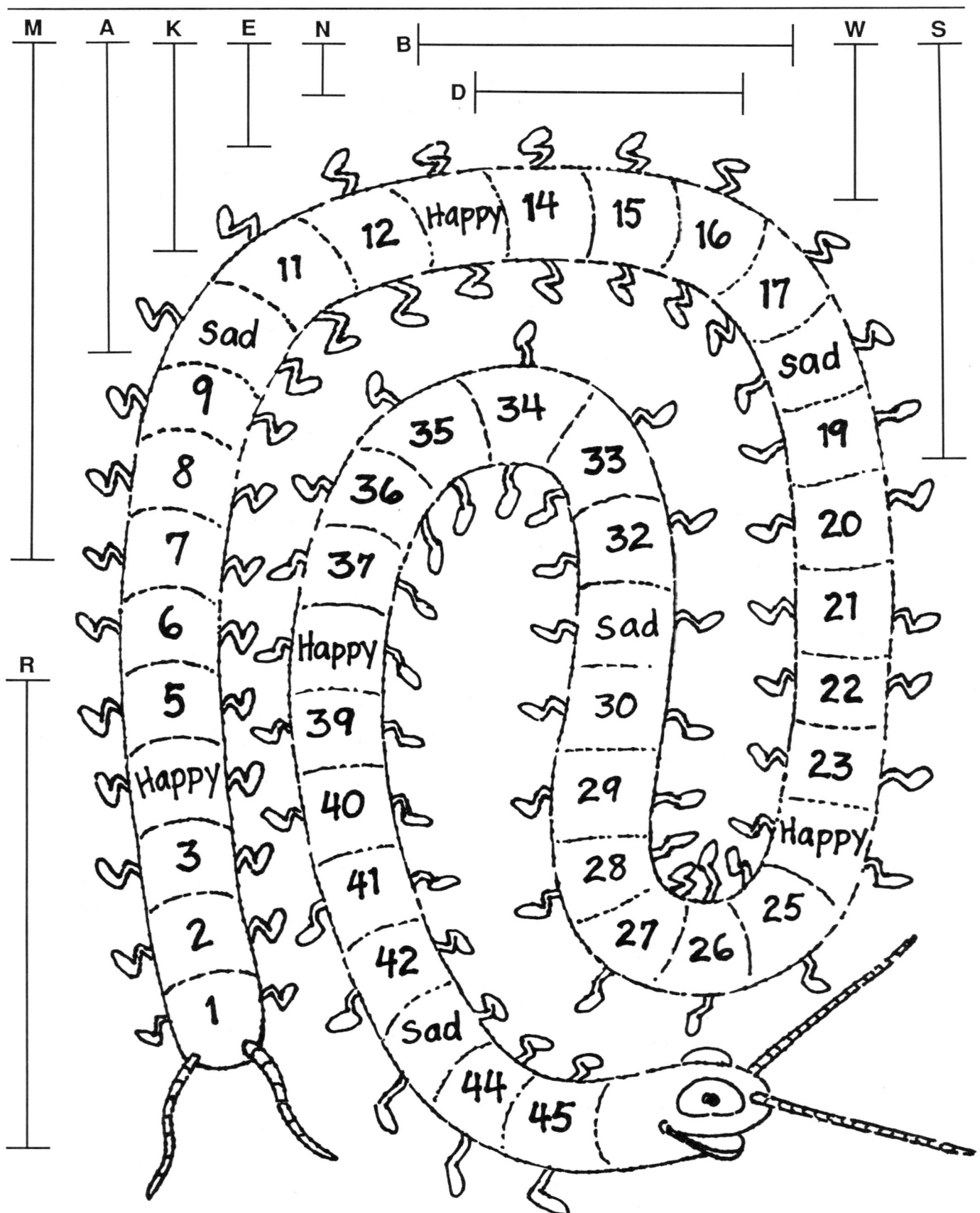

The Centimeter Crawl (2)

GO AHEAD the number of centimeters in line segment **A**	**GO AHEAD** the number of centimeters in line segment **K**	**GO BACK** the number of centimeters in line segment **A**	**GO BACK** the number of centimeters in line segment **K**
GO AHEAD the number of centimeters in line segment **B**	**GO AHEAD** the number of centimeters in line segment **M**	**GO BACK** the number of centimeters in line segment **B**	**GO BACK** the number of centimeters in line segment **M**
GO AHEAD the number of centimeters in line segment **N**	**GO AHEAD** the number of centimeters in line segment **S**	**GO BACK** the number of centimeters in line segment **N**	**GO BACK** the number of centimeters in line segment **S**
GO AHEAD the number of centimeters in line segment **E**	**GO AHEAD** the number of centimeters in line segment **D**	**GO BACK** the number of centimeters in line segment **E**	**GO BACK** the number of centimeters in line segment **D**
GO AHEAD the number of centimeters in line segment **R**	**GO AHEAD** the number of centimeters in line segment **W**	**GO BACK** the number of centimeters in line segment **R**	**GO BACK** the number of centimeters in line segment **W**

The Liter

Waltz tempo

We know a me - tric u - nit of length. It's called the cen - ti - me - ter.____ And now to mea - sure things that we pour, we'll learn { to use the li - ter.____ A
{ a - bout

Note to Teachers

Linear measurement is usually studied before other kinds of measurement, so the beginning of this song about the liter reviews the centimeter.

The liter is a unit of liquid measure with somewhat less capacity than a quart. We know that we divide a quart into two pints or four cups. To divide the liter similarly, we divide it into two half-liters, each of which is a little less than a pint. We also divide the liter into four "metric cups," two per half-liter. Each metric cup holds a little less than our customary cup.

With this in mind, the lines of the song tell us that "a liter will match with two half-liters, or we also can match it with metric cups four."

To help the children remember the metric unit for measuring liquid, the song ends with "Think: Liquid! Metric! Liter!"

li - ter will match with two half - li - ters, or, we al - so can match it with me - tric cups, four. When

mea - suring li - quids like fruit juice or milk, think: Li - quid! Me - tric! Li - ter!

Quarts, Pints, and Cups

Brightly

Note to Teachers

This little song about the U.S. standard units for measuring liquids—quarts, pints and cups—is really a mnemonic device. It helps students remember the relationships between these units. The sequences 1, 2, 3 and 2, 4, 6 are easy to remember. Since there are two pints for every quart and also two cups for every pint, the song states the rate briefly and clearly.

♪ The use of tables is one method of problem solving recommended in the National Council of Teachers of Mathematics (NCTM) K-12 Curriculum Standards (1989). Have students complete the tables on the *Quarts, Pints and Cups* Student Worksheet (page 92) and use them to solve the problems on the sheets. Remember to use the song to review the concepts.

♪ Teach older students this second verse: "If gallon's 1, 2, 3, half-gallon's 2, 4, 6. Half-gallon's 1, 2, 3, then quart is 2, 4, 6," and so on. Use the Student Worksheet on page 93 with these students. Create more problems that they can solve using the table.

Quarts, Pints, and Cups

Complete these tables:

Quarts	1	2	3	4	5	6	7	8	9	10
Pints	2	4	6							

Pints	1	2	3	4	5	6	7	8	9	10
Cups	2	4	6							

1. Judy is having a party. She needs 14 pints of ice cream.
   How many quarts should she buy? _____

2. Kim made 8 pints of lemonade to sell.
   • How many cups does she have? _____
   • If she sold them all at 10 cents for each cup, how
     much money would she take in? _____
   • Could you solve the last problem by making a table? Try:

Cups	1									
Cents ¢	10									

3. You can buy 5 pieces of candy for a penny.
   How many can you buy for 10¢? Complete the table below to find out.

Cost of Candy	1¢	2¢	3¢	4¢	5¢	6¢	7¢	8¢	9¢	10¢
Pieces of Candy	5	10								

     Teaching Primary Math with Music © Dale Seymour Publications

Gallons, Quarts, Pints, and Cups

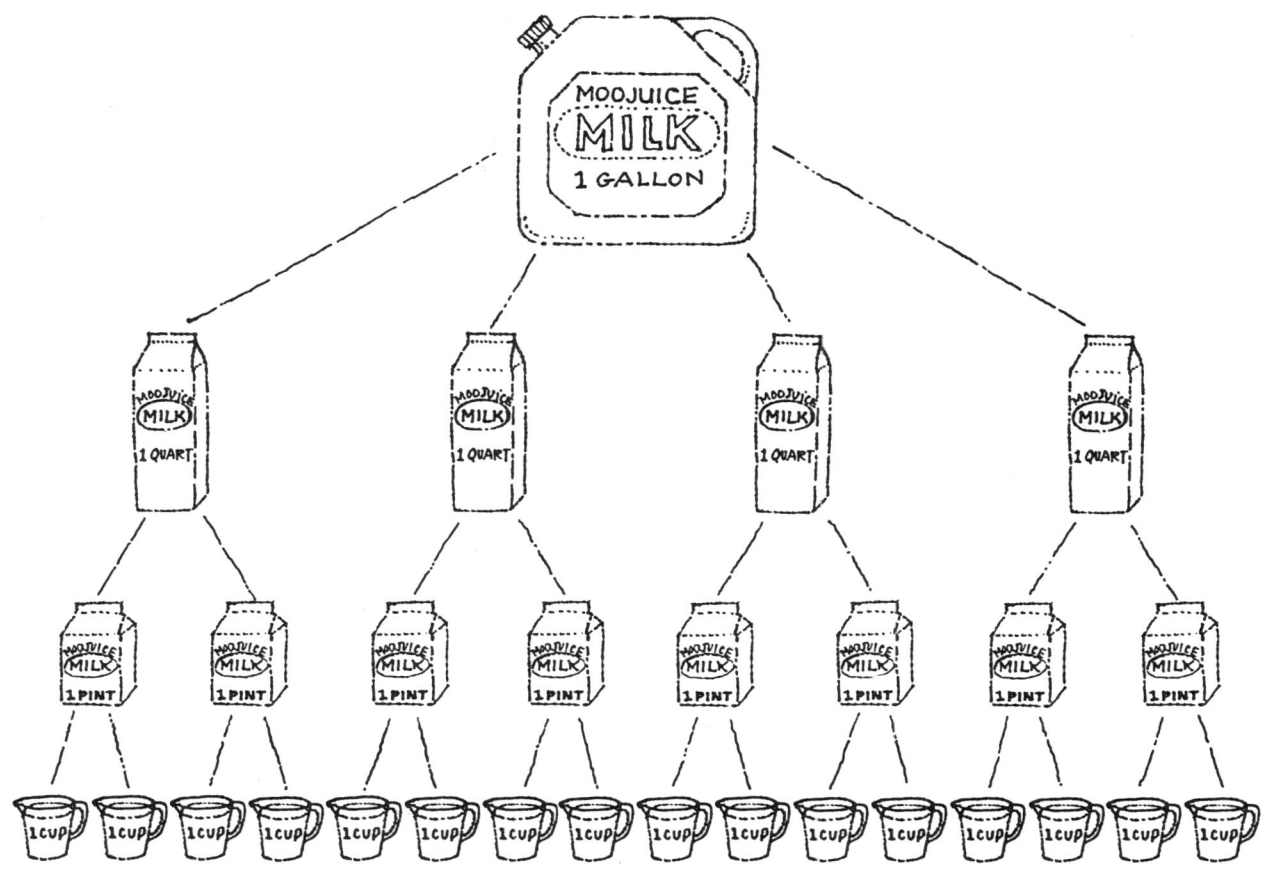

Fill in the table to show the number of cups, pints, and quarts there are for each gallon:

gallons	1	2	3	4	5	6	7	8	9	10
quarts	4									
pints	8									
cups	16									

Use the table to solve this problem:

John is planning a picnic and figures he will need 128 cups of punch. How many gallons of punch should he make?